Hard Candy

Hard Candy

poems by

Jill Battson

INSOMNIAC PRESS

Edited by Mike O'Connor
Copy edited by Sandra Dawson & Liz Thorpe
Designed by Mike O'Connor

Canadian Cataloguing in Publication Data

Battson, Jill
     Hard Candy

Poems.
ISBN 1-895837-01-4

I. Title.

PS8553.A8336H3   1997   C813'.54 C96-932451-0
PR9199.3.B37H3   1997

Printed and bound in Canada

Insomniac Press
378 Delaware Ave.
Toronto, Ontario, Canada, M6H 2T8

This book is dedicated to the memory of my dog Fungus, my constant companion for 14 years, whose unconditional love and unjudgemental listening made the creative process bearable

Special thanks to:
A.M. Allcott, Waheeda Harris, Kurt Heintz, Bob Holman, Adeena Karasick, Mike O'Connor, Stan Rogal, James Spyker, Sean Southey and to the memory of Greg Good, Isaura Silva, Ian Stephens and Andy Zysman.

Thanks to:
Wolsak and Wynn, TSAR Publications, ARC and Descant whose recommendations triggered income. And the Toronto Arts Council, Ontario Arts Council and Canada Council who all gave me money to pay my Visa bills over the last several years thus allowing me time to write most of the poems in this book.

Extra special thanks and gratitude to Steve Tamasi.

Contents

Cough Candy

Glacier Mints

Salt-Water Taffy

Aniseed Balls

Death of a Loved One

Too soon to know the medley of pain
but the hints are there
that wrenching feeling in the hollow of my heart
appetite that makes the stomach heave
time will heal
and other cliches
time makes it more real
time stretching out in front
an eternity to healing, to forgetting
switchblade in the gut
and those painted rooms yawning for life
the bed an ocean of emptiness
what alone really means
cibachrome emulsive shrine aide-mémoire to abet
but the futility of life shines through
with every relax hot bath
every haunting jazz song
want the blossom fullness of wine in the mouth
the tylenol hum
to run my hands over you once again
the thought of this
pricks my eyes salty reminiscence
one of my arms torn off
my abdomen devoid of anything but space
constant chest tightness
you were the part of me that kept everything whole
and here I go again
weeping.

Butterscotch

Back Love

And this is the way it happens
with a herniated disc
as the knife cuts through soft skin
deeply through thick musculature that keeps one upright
into the recesses of paleozoic bony structure spine
to release the grape-size problem
and it happens like this in love too
the knife of emotion, of need, of want
slices through to the heart
the centre of all feeling, the very point where
duodenum meets stomach
or any place else the body locates the imagined feeling
tingling pain, yet not pain
made raw and real by love
and this is where the grape of discontent harbours itself
somewhere in the central cavity of the body
a seed that grows with every sharp word
every hand not held, every promise not met
every night left lonely
until it festers to its full dimensions
an annulus of cartilage
wreaking havoc on the nerves
until the body can no longer stand the repercussions
the growing dysfunction in months of pain
constant hope that tomorrow things will be better
in both cases
surgery becomes the only way out.

Skinny Dipping

The new sensation
extra coldness of water on expanses of the body
usually covered with spandex, lycra
I swim out into the reed weary lake
the sun weaving and dipping behind clouds
copper water alive with tiny fragments of sediment
glowing rust over the sudden white of my body
my breasts buoyant as you take the hardened nipple in your mouth
you hold me close, laying your cheek on my chest
and we cling to each other floating in the mirrored softness
I am wet in wetness as your hand traces the contours of ecstasy
our skins rippling with goose pimples of early summer
the lake is quiet
save the blue heron flapping across surfaces to new grounds
if there are people observing us, we do not feel them
we are alive only for each other
mouth to mouth in the iron/wood fragrance of the water.

Degrazzia

It has been 20 days since the last time
I looked out over your property
sun-warmed
divided
squinting under Tucson skies
familiar adobe brick radiating warmth
into the square of the courtyard

I came here years ago
travelled for weeks
rescued in minutes
tequila burned like gasoline in my throat
gazing with urban high-rise eyes
over alien southern terrain
pocked by cholla
smoothed by terracotta

I loved you from that moment
grey in your beard
picked out by the sun
like a shiny reflection on black
you waved from the driver's seat
of the 50's Ford
which, like you, never rusted
gloss blown off years ago
by hot winds and desert rain

It has been 20 days since I drew my fingers
for the last time
over the mexican leather of your face
remembered how
I sliced cactus with a
carbon axe that jumped in my hands
carried water in leather buckets
to build your dream
steadied the base of hand-lashed ladder

pressed my face into the back of your legs
cotton with patina of yellow brown
dirt smooth from a thousand hand wipes
familiar reek, the oil of your flesh
cast aside my white woman's ways
learned the soft tortilla of your palate
hot peppers I tasted with your skin
debated eating the worm

Christ and the sun in fluted shafts
crashing between beams
of an open-roofed chapel
I spied through wooden cracks
to watch you pray
see manifested the pious discipline
zealot of your own religions
the bubbling envy that kept me pure
beat in temples
forced me to walk out from your shadow
to the sun of separation
and for 20 days have wished I never left.

Kathy

I burnt the ridges of my fingerprints smooth
when I touched the sun of your face
sulphuric acid of the Kray brothers
my kneecaps nailed to the floorboards of life
bending forward I peered through
a knot-hole down to the cellar
to see your beautifully shaped shaved head
hiding from the husband who raped you
broom handle, broken wine bottle
caught wearing your dresses
you suggest he shave his armpits
tasted the sharpness of your own blood
back of hand contacts smart mouth
I bought you a green felt hat
to keep your skull warm in winter
protect you from his frigidaire gaze
frail body gave softly under my thumbs
I wanted to heal you
I tried everything, gave you the love you craved
wrapped my body around yours wracked with sobs
held you against my breast
alone in the cellar you hug your knees tight
my old grey dress strains over them
we are forced apart
I am unable to free my knees.

Circus

Sometimes I am a circus
and you are my fat lady
awash with Melville's legend
and the sweat of a thousand sexual encounters with
sideshow freaks and red dwarfs
that whoop and carouse inside me
when I travel long distances in my car that has no radio

Fat lady, you are my double Adonis
twice wider and deeper than I want to be
you loll outside my trailer peeling grapes
on an upturned orange crate
groaning under your weight
while I secretly thumb through inky personals
looking to replace you with
a bearded lady, a tattooed lady
in my room stark and neat
books alphabetically filed
bedding hidden behind fake wood panelling
on which a postcard of Leonardo's Cartoon is tacked
perfectly symmetrical to the grooves in the pressed sawdust

My billet immaculate as yours is Dionysian
empty wine bottles strewn
suspended eternal leaves of typewriter paper
concertina solidly in air heavy with the aroma of
fermenting fruit
warmed by candles of sculpted grease and glass
kitchen knife twangs in the wall
next to a dishevelled bed
heavily indented with your form

I heave when I am there
smothered by chaos and the bacchanal stickiness
of your breast
sandaled feet crunch sawdust

liberating cedar oil scents
confined to ankle height by the atmosphere of the room

My spine aches from the pressure of you
one day I will buy a car radio
flee the circus
live a normal life, devoid of you
— interloper of my interior monologue
but for now I am a circus

The newspaper hidden
crushed beside you on the crate
fleshy arm about my shoulders
siamising me into you
I feel the rasping, sweet liquid roll
of the peeled grape
across my reluctant tongue.

C with S

This is the way we view things
through the silver-darkened glass of mystery
ocean-warmed seaweed
a floating membrane in the body of salt
finality of purple swirls
marks the beginning
the mirror glinting in a lazy Cocteau fantasy
tilting over water, under sky
every sense enhanced
fragrance of gardenia, the particular glaze of saline
each capillary a maze of sensations
the mirror reflecting a crush of crimson overlaid with lead
final rush of softened smoothness
in the heaviness of limbs
the silver-darkened glass closes to black.

Home from the Poetry Wars

for BH

Holman,
it is you that soothes the tempest
appears in airports to carry the bags of distrust
unrolls the carpet of opportunity
pumps the pillow of satisfaction
feeds me the warm milk of warriors

Holman,
it is you that brings me home
lays out the message on the counterpane
soaks me in the scented waters of what has gone before
rubs in the balm of what will always be
cleanses me from the grime of the poetry wars.

Spearmint Pips

Waiting

A calmness has settled over me
the patience of Job
moon, blood impacts each differently
two are effected
one affected
there is a time schedule that dictates all hormonal
whacked out on Larium
the quinine crawling towards Friday
in this house we play three-way control
to nothing
the schizophrenic arrangements
run tally through doors
out of each of our hands
and then we three sit stupefied, waiting
the focus has shifted
today I am calm
even you don't bother me
cyberspace can wait in the wings
and I am focused on a life of contentment
the crawling doubts can live tomorrow
moon shifts towards full
the water in our collective body responds.

Monday Afternoon

In a slash of sunlight
on a sun-starved, warmth-starved place
I am mine
and all is flash and glitter
a mouth of words
dangerous and forgiving
breeze on me
the mild wind of exigency.

174 Chances

And then there is this
the mucal substance between our thumb and index finger
stretching away against the biological countdown
to the next millennium
snappy or loose dictates who we are
what we could be
smaller than a fetus it sticks against mucosal membrane
positioning as placenta developer
harvester of blood, collector of genetic citizenships
resting, almost, to decide if souls live here
...if this is my soul
weeks later reflecting torpor
it gives up the ghost and flushes hope and excitement
reading despair behind the eyes
to the core of the body where no person sees
not even the mind of the host
the will of somebody's god
or an equally uncontrollable force
of nature
him/her/it
we collectively count the days
caught up in a cycle of hormonal fixation
like there is no tomorrow
and there are very few tomorrows before anticipation empties
into the heat of remembrance/regrets
we are divided exactly
in this house of spirits
there are two fertilities a month here
fourteen days separate individual ideals
essentially identical in the development/outcome
we catch it up in our fingers
taste the metallic lifeforce that cushions delivery
I pose questions to the tired audience of one
what lives in the deepest part of me
and can it be fooled by plain desire
this is the reason for the virtue of patience

my whole questioning is answered
in the process which cannot be rushed
the long haul dictated by nothing
and that is why the millennium swells seemingly nearer
with every thinning mucus finger snap
the brown stain of age bookends the crimson rejection
one instance of hope in half a lifetime
we join the countdown cognizantly
near the end of wasted time.

Fallopio

Twisting, raw scraping
promise of life
and the shedding of it
fertile, bright
a tree reaching for
fruits held for a lifetime
water creature waving filaments
young and supple
breadth of hips means everything
unwalking nation
of childbearing illusion
translucent pink
and hard red threads
three square
most fertile land of the grey
blood rich, eager to cushion, to nourish
spongy tissue
risks shaft, the exquisite pain
pheromone wafts fertility
the smell of procreation
is heavy in the air tonight.

Time and Tide

Sucking and tearing
my safe home
is contracting me into the world
body of water from a body of water
expel me from the sea of evolution
into a cold world from which I hanker to return
skinned rabbits and I
have much in common
my soft bones and I are easily impressed
four sections of my skull
as tender as wind-blown curtains
I am dressed in swaddling bands
restrained pupa in bloodstained cloth
among the trash of a trawled ocean
lucky to find land
when others have kissed cold porcelain
or smothered in the plastic blackness of garbage
I am surrounded by the characters of my indifference
and little silver fishes
whose bodies, excited and fluted
flap against my bound self
the forgotten trauma
birth with death.

Desert Woman

for two voices

Swooping in over another picked clean carcass
vulture glides in
opening closing claws feet around spine
        somewhere under her knee a fragment
        seashell-shaped fragment
        holey bone pinches flesh
catwalking old life spine to skull
        she bears it
ground is live
security in death
sun's energy heatwaving out of the desert
        she sits
        absorbing the heat of the land
shimmering over hot granite
        noontime land
        bone into flesh pinching
        heat soaking into thigh bones
rocking the bird into myriad oily colours
        into ball and socket
        arcing between legs
        in a heat energy horizon
tortoiseshell quality of horn
geographic wafers of cells
        obligation to invoke desire gone
splitting away from lubrication
        so much heat here
        feels like the inside of her
        heat relaxes lungs and mind.

Pear Drops

Pugilistic Relationship

Negotiating each other
in lumbering movements
of pumped muscle cut on rarefied bones
steady, deliberate
moving aggression
into slick arms of the opponent
with a muscle-clinched sigh
they are home in each other's embrace
knowing their rivalled big inches by hard work and pain
resting foreheads, rub of hair over skin
the salt sweat burning
grasping each other, like lovers
their arms pour over the body
down backs or across deltoid patterns
with a caring caress
cheek to cheek
slow dance of the rhythmic
          because heavyweight boxing and love are so similar
jab that takes seconds in the life of the ring
to connect tissue
whiplash back neck on thick architecture
brain cascades against skull
a spray of sweat crystalling out
and this is where brain damage occurs
on the red ropes of the ring
pushed back by the slow, deadly, expected punch
a sleepwalker's cognizance that nothing matters
beyond this moment
when gloves come up, punching air
in a stunned arc that never connects
never protects
and the eyes: split, closed, blinded
see nothing past this fragment
this anticipated pain
living only in the hot spangled lights, the roar of the crowd
taste of blood in the mouth
the stolen electricity of defeat.

Negligence

Holding on for the moment you turn outwards
I crash upon the world
with the weight of all decisions
lips heavy with responsibility
           I am grasses grown tall from neglect
                without breath's caress my skin grows thick
                    membranes seal eyes and ears
I want to feel companioned
but your tongue, cut out,
would make a tasty totem to your specific muteness
           I rebel in silence
                cutting caring signals
                    damaged in ways never audible
I am the very way your heart beats.

Whispered Lament

If I could pick olives on an island made of you
it would stop the density in my head
a billion stars twinkling in an uneven atmosphere
tubular hollowality of sound
turns slowly in a paper rustle of wind
       the lake — swell and slap on anything solid
only here can you recognize a whisper
hold a wind message behind your ear
       as alder leaves rock to ground
we, dreaming every frond
a thousand stems rustling your name
whispers you as I heard you first
telling me gawk and green peppers
a thousand wooden pawns rumbling through your hands
catching on the once gold ring, knocking
the reeds whispering up new dreams
breathing over my eyelids, in bed, in sleep
       Holman sleeping rough on a picnic table in Tokyo
and me telling you everything you missed
contained in the attitude of spruce pointing down
       half-blasted pine whiteboned to sky and river
your breath captured in the smell of lakes

and if I had a cherry pit for every time
you said you loved me
I could live in a vast orchard the rest of my days
by now bearing fruit.

In the Shadow of Things to Come

I'm thinking back to a year ago
the interior of the black stretch limo
threading itself up post rush hour Don Valley Parkway
we are listening to J. tell queer stories
in a tranquillizer drawl
the trees have the dark green foliage
that precedes autumn colour
exhausting their chlorophyll to the closing days
A. is here in spirit on creaking black leather
and we pull darkly into the funeral home
all hands outreached to steady J.
the family waiting room sombre
plush hardness, a room to faint in
I wait there while the others view the body
hands under J.'s arms to hold him up
gets his Leica out, clicks a last photograph
macabre death-mask shot
and I am there for everybody
the diamond on my finger lest I should forget
tied to this family in sickness and in health
Paul is the first one out of there
after the depressingly, thankfully short service
invisible as in life inside the red wood box

At the cemetery the plot is gaping, waiting
right against the perimeter fence
shaded by dense shadows of the apartment buildings
not exactly a location Paul would choose to spend eternity
a man who loved roses and deserts and opera
J. is greyer than concrete
staggers slightly walking squiffy along muddy grass
a late September day
high holidays loom
on the eve of Rosh Hashanah
a chill wind laces the drizzle
and boiled eggs are forced upon me by the dozen

eat and celebrate life
M. is torn between grief and sociability
a daze of the last 24 hours and trying to help him is impossible
so numb, so numb
the internment is over in minutes
and we are shushed away from the grave
even though I want to stay until the end
as is customary with me
I am hurried back to the limo
my palms on the back of M., of J.
anticipate the journey back to the hospital
eat eggs and kosher chicken in J.'s room
the drugs keeping him level
we are awaiting the grief

it's so traumatic, all this loss in such a compacted time
a year later and I'm sweating in Africa
thinking about M.; that plot next to Paul's
and when J. will be in it
I'm thinking how I might never know
and if I did, would I turn up
to stand at the back of the funeral home without the diamond
just one of all the other people giving respect
would I take M. in my arms
because nobody was there to polish his shoes before this funeral
because I know what's coming
his freedom and responsibility clashing in one single day
the ending of one, beginning of another
meeting over grass a year apart
and everything I have to say is bound up in the here and now
I'm thinking I should see him when I get back
despite rankle and anger, grief is what kept us
and I was giving into a void
all this history, our lives marked by the funerals we've attended
the impossibility of this time we spent in each other's pockets
and why he never loved me enough.

Sometime After the Third Time

I am surfacing, like in an Atwood novel, surfacing
from a larger oppression, insidious and life consuming
I am bobbing to the surface
face gleaming with the water of discontent
to be pushed under again by circumstance
a thousand salty knives pushed into flesh already raw
it is when I come up a third time
gasping for the air of salvation
that you face me in all your glory
a man for whom it seems I have waited sixteen years
sudden leap of faith into your arms
a score of poems written in your honour
love so raw and tangible that weeping does it no justice
when you open your arms to me the world metes out liberation
to hold my cheek against the expanse of your chest
makes me feel
        everything is all right
        outta sight
I can only use words in poetry that spell the real meaning of you
but these words apparently mean nothing
in the vaulted universe of our lives
this is where the poems end
and with it the nights where nothing existed save
plastic discs priding themselves
the touch of fingers on skin, like those thousand knives reversing
themselves
into a blooming of passion
but for every surfacing there is a drowning
        and here is mine:
when I leave the house to get the weekend papers
and blueberries for our breakfast
I return to find everything you own is gone
whisked away in several nylon bags
and you are too, without a note of explanation
a kiss to tell me where you are
when or if you'll return

and this is the third time in as many weeks
that I walk in the door to find this emptiness
oesophagus kisses duodenum kisses stomach kisses heart
the water closes in over me
a definite panic
as my life-warmed face feels the creep of water beside jaw.

Relationship

for Jay

Experience nothing outside your own experience
and tell me they were the best of times
bright and clarified
I remember next to nothing
leaded memory box
safely shuttled away behind eyes
but you remember everything
smash it into two failed marriages
a son with your same eyebrows and cowlick
melancholic unhappiness
and then at four year intervals
compelled and wavery-lipped
remind me
how much I taught you
how perfect it was
and how I fucked up your life.

Shark Kills Two

Craving the independence of being alone/I stay on in Hong Kong/to experience the alone of alone in a crowd of five million/when I achieve it I become lonely/discover the difference between lonely and alone.

Knowing that when I return to Tokyo I will hate him anew/not really care if we end because everything about him betrays me/betray and betroth lay together.

Shark kills again in Hong Kong harbour/in Sydney shark kills two/the territorial range of sharks moves into the unconscious/I dreamt of him last night/gums red and blood-filled/tiny marble black eyes pushed deep into jade chinese flesh/and then I dreamt of sharks.

Humbugs

June 27th 1996

Mac's smokily repressed voice booms out over a seated audience
the bluing night a yellow glow of candles
white waxiness bears an interior gold pulse
over two thousand names illustrate an iceberg tip
in the cold waters of destiny
I am thinking how unbearably beautiful this candlelight tribute is
the summer reading of names, official yearly memory
greg good, isaura silva, ian stephens
and others not as close, but dead none the less
the landscape of the living shifts
melts away like hot wax, a ralph steadman drawing

then the feeling of you under my palms
geographic textural diversity in a few square inches
the skin on your shoulders almost hairless, smooth like mine
all this my life is rooted in, the promise of existence
for a touch of your mouth
the careful way you wipe semen from my legs
watch me wash when metal staples prevent bathing

hold my face in your hands again
as I remember my dead
the nonplussed questioning, a silent 'why'
story of our young lives, a death build-up
that seems so unreal, so unimagined, so not us
the single truth that family is everywhere and we build it as we see it
mine is here with you now, languorous and calmed
as well as out there in the summer evening park
sharing community in a meadow of candlelight
what would I do now, my hard exterior melting away
under the light of you
a precarious balance of strength and breakdown
the next minute or an hour away
and when I feel it most is when I lie with you
or tonight at this candlelight vigil.

A Morphine Headache

for Isaura

Shout
   there is   of Portuguese
rattling through the kitchen
    and behind that closed
    semi-gloss
    latex newly painted door
a chosen grey
    the billowy softness
of death impending

knocking of rosary beads
tacky   mucus   rattle
in the throat
dice players
on the road to death
    and how much do you charge for snowblowing?
    speak louder
    you paid too much
and she is   toxic   yellow brown
skeletal remains with an ocean view
    and know I do still you
I do

swallow it
just one draught
and you will be talking
    listening to them I am
    at my age I don't give a fuck
cloying urine turns thick
  ahh
    the bed under sometimes it gets stuck
    in the light so I can see you
    kiss me
in a room of ceramic pigs
she is   soft-focus delirium

Fisher-Price alarm   baby crackles
we cut morphine with valium
up and down
sleep and talk
          hand still   blood   warm
with
pressure of   heat   cheek on lips
air kisses   breathless in my ear
there is no depth to the horror
          Jill it's only
          hug me
there it is — I can never do more.

Thrush

Cavernous red the burgundy moistness of speech
house of the poetic, pragmatic
yeast that knows no bread
fermenting, bubbling white
no interference
in this growth
ruptures in softness, ridged concave
root buried deep
hotter than body, cold as snow
feverish pitch the acidity of lemons, of vinegar
103 in the shade of this opening
a complete skin stops only in the roots of the teeth
ulcerated calm flowering of white
delicate bacterial frosting
jack condensates frozen on the window of the living.

Woodbridge Memorial Gardens

for Andy Zysman

Unbroken expanse of astroturf
around a grave gaping open
sides lined with bright green, crackling plasticity
reaching down to meet the open concrete sarcophagus
all the naked, offensive earth shrouded

at the bottom of the pit
sealed into red polished oak
the body of the man I loved
a certain detachment
etching details into the mind's eye
today everything is a reminder
of life left behind

everyone takes a spade full of earth
tips it into the grave
David, his sneakers smeared red with mud
frantically shovels the earth
spade full another spade full
working for a rounded muffled thud
rather than an empty scattering of earth
spinning off glossy wood

I leave the grave
walk up the hill along crazy paving paths
doesn't take long to be alone
upright slabs of granite and marble stretch away
like grey dominoes
the wind is getting up
pushing dampness that will soon be rain
into my face
the graveyard, packed with silent sleepers
perfect venue for private tears
grief is what you do alone

headstones bear a harvest of small rocks and stones
take from the earth and remember
on the tarmac a beautiful red pebble
mesmerizes
root it in my palm
smooth and comforting
warm against hand in pocket

when I return to the grave
staff are clearing away chairs and canopy
a bulldozer, mechanical caretaker
rakes remaining earth gently into the grave
plywood panels scraped and piled
hearse, limousine, family — gone

David and I watch until the very end
until the marker is put into earth
nothing else visible will happen
then I walk over to the mound
eye-popping terracotta against
manicured emerald lawn
and plunge my fist into the pile
arm up to the elbow
and open my hand
leave the red, warm, smooth pebble
embedded in the earth
where it will sink, slowly
unite with the man I loved
dust to dust
become part of the monument
my token forever
because I will never return.

Goodbyes in a Cemetery

You jog through the cemetery, an act of forgetting
maintain there is no closure in you
death barely breaks a sweat in the landscape of your consciousness
it is a ten-kilometre/fifty-five-minute sweat slog

on this occasion I cycle beside you
turned September, the evenings are closing in
it is mere days before I leave the continent
and I yearn to be with you at any hour
share some small act
not missing a second of your breathing beauty

in this cemetery I wrote time on separation
a frosty morning in early January
and I am in black, in black, in black
we rode out the many cars of existence
crowded into the chapel where her coffin echoed silence
fingers, lips on wood, the warm taste of life
pressed burning, lasts the day
stained glass lends a medieval ear to the weeping
and we file past, the last goodbye
out into the marble sarcophagus of the mausoleum
rows of tiny compartments house the urns
of Wong and Finklestein
Smith and Mulange
and we are squeezed out into the breath cutting morning
right at this very spot on the pink stone gravel where you pass daily

I pause here for a second while you run on
breath the summer air with its tinge of falling leaf autumn
calm my heart
remember her encased within the mausoleum
pig cookie jar and the small objects of her life
surrounding the makeshift urn like an Egyptian
this is a place where I come to remember all the dead of my life
the very silence triggering memory pavlovian

I watch you turn the corner running on
swish crunch of gravel goes on for minutes
this is what I'm leaving
the mirrored point of you
death memories of all things
that leave you untouched
and then I peddle on behind
anxious for the warm hope of my life.

On Remembering Andy

And Jake sits hospital confined
crumpled sheets of blood warm bed
white yellow fluid of bloated abdomen
of tongues
just another Atwood day
blinds closed to a dense head
juniper berries oil the air
of steamy closet rooms

And at home in the closed stillness
tapestries hang for him
waiting motionless, airless
clogged with the dust of days
jagged piles of soft books multiply
black and white of blood work
reflects reality from walls
resigned air of the shiva
shuddering motes and minute particles
all wait for him

And his eyes sunk and hopeless
when I walk into the room
it is the nature of us
holding his hand so decisively, my forearm cramps
grasp of reality, touch of the outside world
always the last time
hard is making it count
we joke about AIDS hair
but he is serious
when day by day chemicals destroy his veins
body collapsing inwards
monitoring death's approach
and after all this mortal suffering
that marks days to the end
I will be the one regretting everything
puckering for the last time
standing watching souls fly out.

Funeral with Jake

Supplicant, I am on my knees
on the black flecked granite floor
it is the 8 a.m. hospital shush
medication trolley twirls its narcotic dance in the corridor
and I am trying to get these god-damned socks
over his useless feet
I am sweating the thin sweat of September
the thin sweat of the terrified
the thin sweat of the majorly hassled
I fetch a hot, wet face-cloth from the bathroom
lay it over his face, pressing my hands down
over his eyes
outlined in their sunkeness by bony sockets
his hair lies flat and greasy over the visible scalp
glinting sickly yellow
he pushes his fingers and water through it
searching for a curl, some curls that will make him look
foppish, rakish
but this man is dying
and no amount of hair will disguise it
I take his arms through silken sleeves
like dressing a baby, takes all my strength
I am a mazola twister pretzel
using the bed, my knees, to dress him
wrap a double windsor under collar
that hangs away from a neck
I could break by touch alone
the ticking voice in my head keeps up the mantra
stay calm, stay calm, stay calm
I help him into jacket black wool that might belong to someone else
and see the desperation mixed with hopelessness
lying dead over his irises
there is a plea there I am too obtuse to interpret
lingering as he leans on my arm to the wheelchair
his sitting bones with no meat on them
sigh into the plastic cushion

and with no effort I push the
chrome and plastic prison
down the hall to the elevator
I watch our reflection distorted and fish-eyed
in the toes of his shoes that I stayed up late last night polishing
as we travel silently floor by floor
sliding down through OR, X-ray, Patient Floors
to the foyer
and the family entirely in black
coverings over hair
limo murmurs in the crescent driveway
we manoeuvre him in through its black door
the black windows hide our grief
we are going to the funeral of Jake's father
dead 23 hours
and then he asks me to go back for his camera.

Questions at the End of AZ

No dementia or faded looks
you did not waste or languish
death's crystalline knowledge
like Satan in a black leather jacket
five days of speculation
and we are New Jersey gathered
thudding of earth
frenetic shovelling of lovers
of friends
and somewhere, muffled yet continuous, a sobbing

> where are the coveted diaries
> the stories of your life
> litany of pain
> physical to familial
> what happened
> those last hours
> when you breathed on your own
> out of exhausted body
> house of the spirit
> physical entity that keeps you here with us
> — the ambulant

scuttling of stones across coffin lid
thudding of earth
on red oak
east coast October is often like this
— warm with a chill and damp
early darkness descending
on darkness within
sooty mist connecting us with you
the questions
one last look.

Greg Again with No Closure

I am
still wondering, a year later
what your last night was like
while I walked home satiated from birthday dinner
the happenings in the weeks between knowing

I am
gliding my fingers raw over your name
at the memorial in Cawthra Park
sensitized to the etch of brilliant metal
reflecting my arm back

I am
in your rooms at the change house studio
tan black stripes and gold brocade
hollow riding boots crack leather cockeyed
missing your touch

I am
looking at photographs
you and Gillian wind-blown
gold hair to white
a person I can't quite remember

I am
at your grave
black marble bench, ashes buried under
butterfly tattoo evaporated
reading a dedication to your perfect hands

I am
seeking closure.

S & I

Last night before the funeral
you were filling my doorway
trying not to leave
the burnt red of your shirt
echoing everything I feel in a second
your need to kiss me
feel validation on my lips

and here I am driving like the devil
to make it on time to Montreal
sit in black on waxy wooden pew
watch everyone remember you
in poetry
you never lose just one
on this trip my dog is newly dead
in the church I'm the only one who can't say a poem
vocal cords and throat melded together
with a mixture of griefs
it is all I can do to stop myself wailing
a theatrical widow nightmare
and afterwards it's the first time I take a drink in months
vodka crashing into my brain
weighting my legs

there was a time when you opened the gentleness of yourself to me
a warm rush of sensations
in the crush blue snow
the very Englishness of you
later that year in the hospital room
your generosity radiating, CMV taking out your sight
there was still Ashley MacIsaac on the cd player and a last story
books and magazines piled high
my dog was still alive then
and I remember thinking how he was the only being
that truly loved me
and you, above all others, would understand that

it would be the last time I saw you
then the call came a month later
and here I am
leaving one love behind
going to bury another.

Bath

And I'm sitting in the steaming tub, thinking how grief is the one great emotion that equals us, that pulls us all together. My grief being no greater, no more real, no more powerful than yours. Hot tears running down my face mingling with sweat and bath water, no salt left now, all cried out over these past three weeks. I'm thinking of Ian who died last Friday and all the friends I've lost in this epidemic. Of Anna who is bereaved, and Marvin who suffers in a mistaken silence to repeat the grief again in a year or so. How pent-up grief causes cancer and I'm afraid of that.

The bath is so hot I am giving up my muscles. Cast back to that time in Tokyo when I became inured to steaming baths. The long soak at the end of the day. Snatched moments in mineral baths in the centre of Tokyo after a day of tourism. Soaked away the grime of seeing. Scalding water reddened my skin. Being the only gaigin in the bath-house and how the women welcomed me, taught me the ritual of bathing that is so central to their lives.

That one afternoon I was squatted on a low plastic stool in front of a pair of taps, soaping myself and sluicing with water. A hot June afternoon, my floral dress and sandals jammed in a locker, the streets outside humid, yet dusty. Not an Evian in sight. Promise of green tea ice cream after the bath. I was washing half-heartedly, waiting for the interest a white woman with tattoos can generate in a room. I stepped gingerly into the bath, the wine stain of heat coursing up my legs into my groin. Hung around the cold water tap for safety. A geisha splashed in, chalk white, with black hair floating out in an impossibly soft arc around her shoulders. Breast-stroked to infinity. She reminded me of the little cosmetic shop that caters to geishas in this neighbourhood where I bought the perfect brush. Temptation of face paint made from nightingale dung, an exotic too rich for my western blood.

The bath was floating steam, filtering up to the peeling painted ceiling, across the tall divider to the men's bath. Me and the geisha were the youngest women in the room. The older women came in traditional kimonos with their many wrapped undergarments. Kimono as Japanese lotus foot. On the side of the bath a woman sat, her profile to me, not fully in the bath or out. She was sobbing. I couldn't see or hear her tears, I knew it in the attitude of her body. Was she crying from grief, loneliness, or the relief of not having to show a stiff upper lip in a room of women? The grief of a thousand handshakes, of a million cooked meals, of a hundred sexual encounters coursing through her, shuddering that slight but age bagged body until I felt the pull of community. I felt no embarrassment or shame, just an in-touch feeling, an I-haven't-been-there-yet, but-soon-will feeling.

The image, burnt on my retina, of that woman has stayed with me over the years. In poems she peeks out asking to be written, to be remembered for her pain, for what she gave me but never knew. And I didn't know either, not until tonight. As I sit in this too hot bath, feeling sick with heat and grief. Our lives so intrinsically bound. I'm doing the same thing. Tears splashing into the water, afraid to sob too loudly in case anyone in my cardboard-walled apartment building hears me. I know why I'm weeping, what my grief is. But after all these years I'm still wondering about hers.

Cough Candy

Fear and Love

for Gwen

Switch bang slap the child
deserted at the side of the road
frighten him to good manners
close up hide-a-bed
with him in it
porky, fat, slit-eyed
brushcut big mouth mummy's boy
fag hanging on the side of her mouth
working ashes to the tip
crumble a grey confetti
into peach cleavage
squinting with smoke
always the red perm
voice stops you at a hundred yards
hard-boiled eggs, black-rimmed yolks
lamb fat in sand-laced sandwiches
the battles
between fear and love
love winning.

Five by Five

Mother sits at table stilled
face a geology of age
rough coarse worked fingers rest
short pile of velour tablecloth
waits for the next five years.

Parasites of Age and History

The story of my father
is the story of the smell of wood
his hard muscle shape
what the parasites of age and history leach from you
and why I never read men through him

      forgetting bends a man
            ancient memories adorn his life
                  air temperature shapes his body

The story of my father
rendered daft by fear
his outer casing shifts and empties
manifold tales disseminated by consequence
beyond hair loss and fading sight
to the core of how we waste our lives

The last remaining story of my father.

Where are the Roadblocks

Different surroundings confuse
enough to scatter dinner tray peas to fetid hospital air
       the police are coming to get you
       refuse all food and drink
       they are poisoning everything
       how did you avoid the roadblocks?
you swear exaggeratedly
it is summer time in England

far from the Tudor cottage
sweetness of Longleat grass on your tongue
lying on your back under
soothing blue of five-mile sky
hardbacked insect navigates your arm
cream squares of sheep
bleating, playing tag
spastic leap into the air when
briefly the walnut brain fries

children will keep you from this
secure your agedness existence
your pound of procreational flesh
buttercups and their secret cache of sweetness
jackrabbit springs over
razor grass
breath screams over it between thumbs
fragility of skylark on high
haunting melody of heather silence
mournful warbling medieval centuries
your orchestra pit of myriad green bracken

new transfixion, new tranquillity
that you must not be alone
or rub between sheets of poly cotton and white
       the police are coming
       nurses with poison
soon you will be soaring like larks
leaping like lambs.

This is My Mother Now

On the high street of a small English town
she slams the shopping bag off her lap and into the street
with a force that is so abnormal, so unusual
the rest of my family goes very still, very quiet
and I seem to be the only one breathing
walking away quickly to be alone

this is my mother
after years of physicality, of doing
confined to a wheelchair

when I arrive back at the car she tries to attack me
arms flailing, shouting and crying from the back seat
she and I are the only ones breathing
and I am holding back an anger close to nausea
as we drive back to my sister's house

where I go immediately to my room
wait for someone to come in and say
it's okay
but nobody does
I am close to saying fuck it
cramming my clothes back into the suitcase and
catching the next flight
home
but something in me says if I leave it
if I leave it
I can kiss my parents goodbye
because this unpredicted rift will never heal

so I go downstairs to where she sits
in a high back upright chair
kneel on the floor beside her
and say look
and say look
and say a whole bunch of other things
I am the grown-up and she the angry child

this is my mother
with five years of pent-up anger
of grief, frustration and depression
and it's all jumbling out in a technicolour mess
before me

captured in her words thrown at me
are the truths of what I don't understand
they echo off my sister half hidden in the doorway
rebound off my mute father
sitting beside us
her frustration at him one of the real aches that nags her
as tangible as the pain of the MS that has taken her out

this is my mother, vomiting up a thousand pains
a hundred lonely nights
at me, the daughter who left
an extended holiday from responsibility
my own life is not a choice
I can be called back
dreading to live that life prescribed in Trollope and Brontë novels
the youngest sister
spinster sister, maiden aunt

and it's three years later when I get the call
I am lying in bed with a new man until noon this Sunday
thinking how great it is to be free
my sister, frail from having to deal with reality
says it's worse than you think, than I thought
and begins to tell me with a voice that speaks my mind
a hollowality that bounces across satellites transatlantic
and I know of the grief she speaks
of my mother and her loneliness
the near hysterical aspects of her psyche
it's time
a niggle of guilt at this freedom from familial responsibility
the pressure of who I owe my life
this is my mother now
and it's time.

Glacier Mints

Seagrapes

Saucer-shaped lush leaves
bow the tree out over the cliff
over the ocean
sucking salt into themselves

Electrified horizon to Cuba
the nightly storm
humidity comes up from the amber earth
softly enclosing me into a capsule of moisture
water within, water without

Last possible moment before dark
the rumble is there, through body
and then blackness, clichéd
velvet, night
the seagrapes' leaves rustling
waves on rocks, fiercer than day
over barnacle corpses
that have countless times bit
into shoe-pampered pad flesh of my foot

Footprint, with toes heavy
softly moulded into the earth
it walks off the patio
houseboy moves around the property
silent, shadowy
colonial fear in me
young man, easy grin, machete
and yellowing eye whites
he has the smell of hard work minus sanitation
heated and rank
flowering into the night like jasmine

And in my room under starched white sheet
the smells of the island
filter through glassless, open shutter windows
fresh smoothness of mahogany floors
and my damp, cool nakedness
I will sleep above all experience
lightly and without dreams.

Jamaican Afternoon

Piercing the eye of the tourist
and it is the experience that hurts
boys with broad dark feet
and yellow chipped toenails
the light brown soles
dusty and hugging tarmac
all the propaganda I've heard about slaves
comes true in the shadow that warns you first
there is a dust trail in the rear-view
cut by their eyes fixed on mine
they keep looking
long after the car has sped away
loose gravel spraying up
from the pothole rocky road
hey girlie
hey pretty girlie
and it is the look which disconcerts

I am temporarily at large from the confinement
of palatial homes
discover a
wealth/poverty dichotomy
wider than Los Angeles
it looks me in the eye
whites of the
or sometimes yellowing
or red
reds of the

> And Rastas amble along roads
> their cap-packaged dreads
> snaking lustrelessly down singlet backs
> I've heard some vacationing women only see the airport
> and the hotel room
> Rastas, their schlong and their stash
> euro definition of a Jamaican holiday

and US television pipes its pornography via Florida
we sit transfixed
as if it's the last time we'll see
Bob Barker
Vanna White
in the heat holocaust of Jamaica
outside the beauty, the tragedy of the island
goes on without us

This is the life of privilege
involves locked gates
armed security guards
imported dogs
close-circuit and big screen TV
total removal from the unwashed mass
smoked windows on the Merc
and the false security of
maids and houseboys
guard you with their lives
count on the myth
that you are their salvation
from a Jones Town iron-roof shanty
lose you means this
plus lost television privileges.

Firefly

for Mike O'Connor

Rasp of fingernails catching
green canvas chair
fireflies on martini glass rim
hot enough to make foliage shimmer
shiver below in the valley
illusion as indigo sky pushes down
soft and cool
no windows on the house
just crazy grey white wood shutters
and white linens
lizards climb walls
scuttle over marble
write their lives in the piano room
everything happens
outside of the small rooms
love affairs
thoughts of Marlene
myriad twinkling
cocktails
slam against a tree trunk
with that hazelnut brown wardrobe boy
free again slaves, slave
and red batik floats down.

Painting with Noël

We are up
up on a mountain plateau
                behind
a valley where faint cloud always lingers
tears of the island blown to mist
                in front
a view like no other here
                they say
Captain Morgan intercepted ships from here
spyglass saw
spur of island sink from...
we fancied ourselves painters
                up here
the breeze in such that
we bend close to hear each other breathe
hear the rasp of sable on paper
fingers on...
                Noël said
Ian, I have found my home
when I die...
best are the island boys
there is no Europeaness with them
tasted our wine
frolicked for us down on the...
their leanness
chocolate ropes of muscle
sweet pink tongues
the paralyzing delight
it is such that
we can only paint black sticks...
and at night
we lay down with the fireflies
smell the salt of Cuba
turpentine of our hands
and in our mind's golden eye
soft white marble over turquoise sea.

Wedding Rehearsal

I'm standing here and I'm standing here and
I'm standing here and I'm standing here and
I'm standing here and I'm standing here and
I'm standing here inside a brown shuttered church
that looks like a Trenchtown shack from the outside
and I'm on the inside I'm on the inside
I'm standing here and I'm standing here and
I'm standing next to him like I'm the best man
bearing witness can I get a witness can I get a witness and
I'm standing here and I'm standing here and
I'm standing with his parents his tense parents and
nothing I say is funny and I'm standing with his tense parents and
this wedding means everything to them means everything to them
means everything to his tense parents and I'm standing here
with his tense parents this wedding means everything to them
the jewel of existence paragon of parental power
I'm standing here and I'm standing here and
I'm standing next to him like I'm the best man bearing witness
with his tense parents bearing witness and it's no joke
it's practice it's practice it's practice it's practice
it's just practice for crying at the church on the day
it's just practice for life.

Salt-Water Taffy

Hitching

This is a story that involves running from a dominant father
California, Key West
touches of unwelcome male hands on your jock 18-year-old body
the man with the B&D suitcase
you handcuffed to the bed that night in Pennsylvania
when it was minus 2 out and all you had on
was a Blue Jays windbreaker
and the wind whistled through that like
no tomorrow
rolling the man for his wallet and car keys
driving to New Orleans for Mardi Gras
the big-breasted woman naked to her waist
dancing to the southern blues
on the balcony below you
disgusting your virginal sensibilities with their size and volatility
Key West
the red-spotted bandanna close to your eyelids
volleyball on the beach, smoking hash and
drinking long island iced tea
into the night with the Cuban hustler
who had 3 ounces of gold hoop in his earlobe
and that afternoon you met Tennessee Williams
a sad softened man with a penchant for morning martinis
never writing a thing after 1978
the girl who left her station behind the bar
walked up to you and dragged her warm pussy along the
blonde hairs of your suntanned, hitchhiking hard leg
before kissing you full on the mouth
just to feel your surprise
and the vacant-eyed man with ten dollars to his name
who fixed you up with a '79 Malibu and drove with you
to the west coast
where the summer of love was still in full swing
yes, this is a story about a dominant father
smacking his wife in the mouth
and you running and running
getting out of the house into the indigo softness and tarmac toughness
of your real world.

Me and Baudelaire

The abject ugliness of sheared off mountain
shale and dust
flags flop flopping over lake
a shadowy blue
and there are clouds this morning
the silver chair of our desire
I am squaw peak'd
dog piss sense of reality
semi-insane social misfits and the vision of that
ebb and flow of shadows across rocks

if only I were here with Baudelaire
him sucking my toes
he could teach me the beauty of barrenness
pines fallen and bleached by pain
snapped off limbs, open carcasses
snow left dirty, smogged like us
our cynic-ness a quality known only to ourselves

and although we feel like gods
we are not at peace here
businessmen carving new slopes with bulldozers
whirring and crashing
this is not our Olympia
me and Baudelaire
perched on a liquid sulphur rock
touching thighs
he is contemplating new muses
since his previous turned to woman

we understand ourselves, each other
cinematographers of poetry
we don't understand shiny Americans
who pick wildflowers in bunches
grasped in oil and economic hands
Hi-8 video cam
a scratched reality of history

the light is altitudinal here
Baudelaire, his slightly green hue
rifling for prozac in my bag
dusty glacial earth, the ginko-birchness
we are bored, perverse and desperate for attention
normality of our thin lives
middle class without the margins

Baudelaire shifts starchily towards me
smell of absinthe precedes his kiss
and where it hits misogyny blossoms
the (dis)illusion breaks
it is me; sun soaked pink granite; pines
in a pocket of America.

Motion of Tranquillity

Evening at Lake Baptiste

White moon hangs over
pink iridescence of sky
the lake calms blue to reflective green
its skittering surface
pulled still by moon
a loon calls, crickets speak
and across the lake
silver rawness of birches
soft zig zag reflections in the water
flies bring tension to the surface
creaking of frogs
their dinner dancing
yellow daisy cactus plant
by floating dock
that swells and rocks under duress
from evening speedboat waves.

Grey Gardens

She is weathered by the sun like the grey plank siding
of their Long Island mansion
paint carelessly splashed on the screen door
white and peeling
nothing but promise
she could have done anything
married anyone
when she lived on Park Avenue
millionaires were always asking
faded aristocracy in faded elegance
now she's just plain crazy
came back from New York City in 1952
to care for the mother she loves
mother she hates
mother and lethargy enslaved her

Sea of green
sea of leaves below the balcony
drop a favourite blue silk scarf
and never recover it
could have married Eugene
but mother sent him away
when he asked her
how someone so warm on the telephone
could be so cold in person
that was the end of Eugene
too young for her, anyway
salt humid breeze coming in from the sea
peaking summer turquoise between boughs

Cats run around with eight toes each paw
humbug striped
looking kind of coonish
she was so beautiful at twenty
in the portrait propped cockeyed on the floor
cat squats behind it and she laughs

lays the New York Times on her bed
so another cat can shit there
amidst empty ice-cream containers
and decapitated flowers

The grocery delivery boy comes
and the gardener comes
and some guy called Lenny
in a baseball cap comes
and the Times comes
and somehow everyone gets paid
she feeds her mother corn on the cob
and iced birthday cake
martinis in mason jars
and they sing
— only a rose I bring you

She waltzes through the hall
black lace scarf under the bodice of her swimsuit
makeup heavy from the sixties
ribbons wound round ankles
white shoes
waltzes to loud military marches on the record player
waving an American flag into the dining-room and back
accompanied by mother yelling
— EDIE
from the bedroom above where cats shit
and corn boils on a hot plate
tea for two
duelling gramophones
duelling mother and daughter
and that's the way it's going to be
till someone dies.

Sudden/Dead/Partner

Asheville '96

The cracked indigo of salt-filled clouds
heavy with the fragrance of Cuban jasmine
migraines in over the house

and upstairs I stand sobbing in the steam-filled shower
bony spider creeping out of the mist of my consciousness
I have been weeping for two days
across a continent of green and ash
the picnic-hoard-bruised hillside
remnants of a storm cloud of sulphur, rubber
smell of black puncturing the Hollywood afternoon weariness

      a crimson rush across winter white skin
      water needles flesh

and later, downstairs, the storm booming out over the mountains
garden fresh with the smell of rain
I am wearing your overalls, sawdust powdering my flaring flesh
woody dexterity of sweat and sawmills
and I am clasping you to me
the weeping constant
in the shutter-shaped evening amber light.

Church Fire

Burn another candle for me
in the depth of this fire
smoke billowing around, ashes casting their frail bodies to the wind
it is here I seek redemption, so light the incense
shake it in the bronzed filigree egg
as the flames shoot up and away from the altar
the slaves made us do it, we shouted
the slaves made us do it
our white skins reddening from the heat
but when the caustic smoke is in our nostrils
choking us with its death threat
then we consider running
unearth the newly dead parson
drive over the coffin with our pick-up truck
again and again
burn another candle for my redemption
the altar cloth heavy with my defecation
we drag it along the floor of the sacred cross
stained glass popping with heat and putrefaction
the slaves made us do it, we said
still the ashes fly around us
beneath our feet embers glow with their acid hallucinogenic
like a cheap imitation electric fire
another candle for my redemption
minister,
the slaves made me do it
for I know not what I do.

Cacophony of Silence

The deep phlegmyness in a smoker's conversation as a cigarette end hisses in a half full coke can then imagine the sound of vocal chords raspings like dried out violin cat gut punctuated by metal pendants jingling on stone pendants that results from an arm movement of stubbing out another cigarette and its crackling dry crunching ash and fire sound stubbing out another cigarette then another then another then another then the hiss of a butt hitting the liquid in a half full coke can then the clank of the cover of a metal zippo lighter the rasp of a fingerprint pulling metal flare of a butane flame then another cigarette then another then another phlegmyness rasping jingling crackling crunching hiss clank rasp then another... ahhhhh.

and then there are the sounds I want to hear again.

Peaceable River Project

Peaceable river project
and it is too real
rubber waders to thigh
the line snaps water glistening
cast out fly
Paul slips my name in
with Kristen, Leslie, for his
gruesome video project of the demented
you are my king, my god
I will do anything for you
pimp squeaky virgins lush
powder smooth, no blemishes
schoolgirl smell of long hair
three lakes and frisson
of video monitor
ah, Paul, you thought they'd never finger you
caught up in a moment so delightful
rush of selective importance
America's favourite past-time
of home porn videos
particular narcissus
those glacial blue eyes
with only pinprick pupils
fishermen gone
in canoes downstream
peaceable river project
Paul locked in dock.

Time to Kill

And I'm thinking about the father
who hacked off his son's head
next to the highway
                    that time I was out at Squaw Valley
how it took 13 whacks of the knife
to sever the thing
the other son screaming, running into the woods
his father driving off down the highway
and throwing the head from the window
60 miles an hour, head, soft asphalt, New Mexico sun
                    and the nature of mercy.

Aniseed Balls

Mumbo

It is decided I should take the front space in this plastic shell that holds our destiny. The least important position and, well, this is my first time. The two instructors, both English, both blonde, both tanned, give overlapping directions. Above all, don't panic. I pull the nylon waterproof skirt up over my legs. Up to my waist. Highland fling gone wrong. Secure the braces. Step off the pebble scattered shore, my feet still achingly embossed with their presence, and into the craft. In only three inches of water the kayak sways alarmingly. In only three inches of water you can drown. Don't forget it. Aaron gets in behind me. He is paler than any resident here. His body lean and compact simultaneously. But he has biceps and I don't. That's what counts. We paddle away from shore. I am in total panic. This is it. The day is lost on me. There is no land, no horizon, just the paddle, water and rocking fear. The kayak shifts alarmingly and I see myself trapped under the boat, under the water. Just like on TV. The retinal memory image imprints for the whole journey. My back is like wood. Muscle spasm hell. The red plastic of the kayak, pimply under my hands, is the colour of diluted blood. Mine. Taste the fear in my mouth. Acid dissolves enamel. Green/grey water of deep lake parts with a hiss as we glide through. The air in my nostrils is hot, odourless. Burning lungs. We skirt the island. It is spring in the sub-Sahara and the trees stretch naked to the sky. Jacaranda purple. Awoken by memory. Twisted and gnarled, stunted by heat. Banana tree leaves slice, sway and cut air. Ethiopian slaves. Loin cloths of goat skin. Of Egyptian cotton. And all moves down to the lake, tumbling with the passage of evolution. The architecture of the island humps out of the water. Smooth, beige boulders, rounded by time and fluid. Near the shore the lake is turquoise. Just like the travel book promised. Alien moonscape below the surface, the rocks, beige to pale blue below the water line, house a million fish. A white crab scuttles along rockscape, electric blue flat fish esses through current. Skin burns red. White tee-shirt flattened wet against my skin the blue transparency. Muscle burns as we paddle into the expanse of lake, our destination a small upturned bowl on the horizon. Could I swim to land? Would this kayak, upturned, save me? Fear of deep water. Fear of unknown creatures in deep water. Mid-lake waves crescent onto the side of the kayak. We are moving constantly, side to side. My hips a belly dancer's dream as I move to the motion. Childhood travel sickness comes back to haunt me. The taste of bile. Yellow in my mind's eye. I fall silent with the enormity of the task. Aaron's paddle swooshes and slicks behind me. In left ear. In right ear. Stereo workout. The island grows bigger as the sun rises. Half moon backwards in the other sky, a silver mystic in the deep blue. The skin between thumb, palm and index breaks open. Water into water. The paddle becomes a painful reminder. The island is so near, but doesn't get any nearer. Aaron keeps up a small grunting of exertion. I rest my elbows on my waist, holding the paddle horizontal to the water. Resting the muscles that become increasingly more tired. Fifty strokes. Twenty strokes. We pass an outcropping of rocks. Sentinel to the island. Waiting. Solid. A crocodile watches us with an invisible eye. Fish eagle circles the rocks. A cormorant dives slick into the water. Silent. Throat with fish as it bobs back to the surface. We paddle into the bay, water soft and content. Temperature changes. The sandy beach winks silver. Trees and bougainvillaeas beyond. And then in the last ditch of my final effort, gritting of teeth, facial muscles tense, we scrape the kayak up over insistent pebbles, onto the Mumbo beach. It's then I feel the speed.

Sub-Saharan Dreams of the Southern Cross

Luangwa, October 1996

The moment I walk out across high-gloss parquet
to the shaded concrete verandah
I know I'm home
not in this structure
but out across the eye-squinting memory of African bush
and the heat literally moves me
a restless discomfort shaking me down
shimmering over miles of flat land
and distant hallucinatory mountains
humpback moss green vegetableness
and the air sticks in my chest, dry and oxygen deficient
a sauna's breath of dryness and heat
quaking my lungs
I gulp for life support
feel the perspiration of living evaporate from my skin
hungrily leaving my face like a desert
assimilating my bones
and around me, from this peak
a three hundred and sixty degree of difference
in every place I look
empty water holes from a river
once running shallow and wide in the rains
sand filled with the trail of crocodile tracks
and white as the bleached skulls of buffalo
the cracked hard earth snaking away in desperation
to trees that know the ravages of elephant hunger
seems at noon I am the only animal standing in the sun
which beats to cow me, to stunt my height
and every particle wants my moisture
throat drying, a rasp of satisfaction
to be stupid, or English enough to be away from air conditioning
the shade of darkened, fan-filled rooms

but my DNA cries out to this
a race memory so vivid it sucks the breath from me
the soap salt water pumped from deep wells
does nothing to quench the thirst in my mouth
in my soul
it's like pulling to the roots you never knew
like returning to arms that love you
coming home at Christmas
take the crashing waves and abundant bodies of water
I only want to walk out and drown in them
this is where I want to be, or on any other dry, hot land
with the sun burning my skin in five minutes
the dead air, sharp intense olfactory of animal dung
heat-induced muscle relaxation
replicable nowhere else in my memory
but here on the scorched earth of the forgotten
air suspended basin of Zambia
this is where I feel at home.

Missionaries

Dear God,

I'm like an invalid. They leave me in peace and go about their work.
Amen. I huddle like an ancient with wool cardigan around my shoulders against an unpredictable northern Malawian chill. My thoughts and I alone while industry is all around. The cleaning of the house. Stitching of clothes. Knitting of blankets. The wrath of God is in the house. Easing into colonialism with the dexterity of Job. The curt way she orders servants around. Anger bubbling under her surface. Menopausal scorn. She has a hair trigger. It's the way she looks at you sometimes. My simple words gone astray. A linguistic mistake. It is always the sanctimonious that hide their faults. Belief in God supersedes the belief in human dignity. Higher power the excuse for the way of all things. From house planning to providing food. Maggot-infested cucumbers are the will of God. So is AIDS. And miscarriage. We are all subject to the will of God. We thank you, Lord, for our daily bread. Amen. There are junkies roaming the house and too many servants to be decent. Yet the anomaly of faith, decency and belief isn't evident in this squatter's bungalow. Paint peeling. Fingerprints on the walls. Cleanliness is next to. Orange dust of the land permeating everything. Rugs. Mosquito nets. The neck of my tee-shirt. As a matter of course you must expect servants to steal. All blacks are suspect. Everyone's clothes are dingy and light worn. My suntan came off in the shower last night. The dogs are coated in the dust. I am reluctant to pat them because it lays on my palms. A coating of grime. The cats are flea-bitten, scrawny, archaic. The animals want to be with me. Or on me. I am St. Francis. I saw a tick jumping over my leg. Its heat sensor turned up high. I check my scalp and body nightly for parasites. This will make me a better person. Humility. Hallelujah. I could live in a New York rat trap now. No problemo. Inured to bedbugs and maggots as I have become. It's only 8:45 in the morning. The day stretches ahead of me interminably. A procrastinator's nightmare. All I can do is write, huddle and wait for redemption in the shape of a good samaritan. Amen.

Initiation Ceremony

We are hurtling along goat-filled mountain roads
the colour of honey
bus gripping lifelike to the asphalt
at 120 clicks per hour
up here the highlands are a forest of spruce and pine
the evergreen population unmolested
green allotments pocket oval between hills
a secret moist cache between deserts
and the bus sweats indigenously
calm broken by crazy lounge tunes of
       The hills are alive with the sound of music
louder than our ears can stand
we are bleeding to country and western
to the southern blues
as I am offered Fanta for the fourth time
a girl in an outlandish frilly sky-blue nylon dance number dress
sits across the aisle
her skin satin, black as the sun gets
startled hair growing out from Banda
and she is hit on several times this ride
by men old enough to know the threat of disease
to which she smiles the eleven years
suppressed girlishness
and I refuse the parchment thin ham sandwich
although a tapeworm is appealing
with its automatic, lazy weight loss program
preferring my three dollar crunchie bar from the hotel gift shop
and she is going to her own funeral, this girl
they say here that semen is rich in vitamin K and D
sex is good for its nutritional value
a patriarchal hybrid corn
and right in my ear the uvular sped-up female singer laments
       If teardrops were pennies and heartbreaks were gold
this girl in her white patent shoes
collecting future gold
en route to initiation into womanhood

stagecoach overland express bus treat
takes Mzuzu in four-and-a-half hours
women will choose a man for her
deflower her with three times the age of experience
three times the age of vitamin K and D
all this to avoid familial shame
if she should go to her wedding bed virginal
cry out with the pain of the uninitiated
I want to cry out
rival the annoying tinstress voice
Why are you doing this? Save yourself! Save yourself!
No, let me save you! I'll take you with me to Canada
I'll… and other lines
my imprinted colonial missionary voice wants to splatter
against the grey/burgundy velour landscape of the bus
and she is smiling and smiling
smiling at the white girl appropriate reversed status
at the back of the bus
and we are hurtling into destiny
she and I
along goat-filled roads the colour of honey
     If heartbreaks were gold
the hills *would* be alive with the sound of music
and
the sound of voices
     If heartbreaks were gold, if heartbreaks were gold
the pandemic alone would take this country out of the Third World.

AIDS Ward

I was pouring over handwritten ledgers of the dead and dying with the young homecare worker. The brown spaces between her corn-rowed hair smiled a nervous smile at me. Her eyes never once gave her away. The chapel had the fragrancy of flowers, and somewhere, not quite hidden, the sweet smell of the saint. Outside, the eleven-hour-old day opened into heat. The door wood knocked, pushed aside. She had come to fetch me, this doctor, her grey/blue eyes with an unidentifiable want. Held me with her gaze. We walked close together along the concrete incline, her red floral skirt whispering, the Irish lilt to her voice undeniable. She told me I talked too fast for an American, but I'm English and that is why my speech is garbled. Our feet padded promises into the walkway. There is money, it will come. There is salvation, it will come. There will be drugs. There is a cure. And all the time talking medicalese with that soft tongue pointing sibilants to the lips, clucking gently on soft palate of roof. And I see myself taking her face in my hands for an unknown reason, her slightly oily hair grazing my forefingers in its bobbed way. This hospital is a village, the orange earth a constant in this land. Women sit in groups; alone on the grass and on benches. They are the hub that turns this wheel. They are the guardians for all time, all people. The patience glowing out of them in a collective history of remembering. Against the terracotta of the bricks made from the terracotta of the earth, and the swirling polished grey/yellow concrete, sits this splash of life, of colour. Here are the women who know no boundaries to their colour schemes, who don't know what not to wear, displayed as life itself. And we are passing, she is talking Tumbuka in its sparsest form and the women respond in a smiling, knee-bobbing way, the authority of a doctor rivalling fear of witchcraft. Somewhere in the malnutrition unit a baby wails and the heads swivel, we are forgotten in their purpose and her hand pushes softly against the weathered wood of the ward door, oiled by a thousand palms, a plethora of fingers. The Howard Hughesian lies in all of us. And especially in me. Go in peace. The air rushes round us like a compulsive lover asking questions. It is a fish tank's air. It is the air that keeps us warm in an ocean. It is exactly the same temperature as the air outside. We are in the calm centre of a collective tornado and there is no antiseptic smell, no comfort in the olfactory. The ward nurse is bright white and crisp as starch, her skin the flawless black chiffon of the young. She leads us into an oblong ward the size of my front room. Pushes a paint-worn trolley containing the tools of the inspection. On the bottom shelf. A yellow plastic bowl with water-sloshing motion. Half a bar of dark pink soap. Ridged. Top shelf. A collection of handwritten reports, white uneven sheets of paper with a tinge of orange from the dust that coats everything. The edges of my fingernails lay testament to the water in which I washed my hands. My doctor tells me we won't use the acronym H. I. V. Instead, we will suggest Immune Suppression. The patients won't be alarmed that way. They won't be stigmatized. A shingle scar will stigmatize anyone, it is a sure sign of the virus. The beds are wide and pink plastic-coated foam rubber. The hospital doesn't supply linens, and all around are hand-knitted blankets, rough grey army blankets and flattened women's skirts. Again the colour of contrast. She doesn't lose that unidentifiable look. When she talks to me her speech has the slow drawl of the possessed. She pauses often. For effect? For clarification? Because she thinks I'm not following all this? The man in the first bed is quiet, laying on his side and recently in possession of a massive stroke. His hair is curled grey, his skin like ashes. He is not the focus, there is nothing much to be done. In the third bed she pushes her white fingers into the soft dark belly flesh of another stroke victim. He is agitating to leave, fully dressed in clothes that have seen better days in the west. She asks him to walk. Swaying slightly he has the asymmetrical face of paralysis. The dark broad feet shift and sink their multitude of bones into the floor. Coming towards me like an omen. In my peripheral coloured cloth pours from beds to floor. The breeze breathes through the room, a sub-Saharan mouthpiece. The occupant of the next bed sits cocky. His face broad and round has the arrogance of the young. Hooded eyes speak sex. The doctor says PCP. She is looking at me in that way. Her mouth relaxed and parted. Time passes infinitesimally. I shuffle the index cards of my brain. Plan the next 40 years of my life. The yellow of her shirt brings to mind the buttercups of my youth, under expectant chins. Do you like butter. Loves me. Loves me not. We move across the room, bowl water expectorates onto the floor in a sparkling arc of life. We all look. Nobody does anything. Papers lift slightly and settle content. He has only one eye and it is sunken in the architecture of his head. On the other side of his face is nothing. I feel my stomach lurch. I don't do eyes, I don't do them easily. The flattened lid, baggy from a recent inhabitant, barely covers the socket and a ruched ridge of pink stares out like a secret. Like a labia. Like a newly discovered love. Her stethoscope warms metal against heartbeat as he breathes for her. Rasping. Disturbed. He has PCP she says and shingles took out his eye. When I draw closer I see the razor marks vertical along the horizon of his lower lungs. Cuts to let the spirit out. Medicine man working his witchcraft. She doesn't say anything. Says everything in her look. I don't speak that language, touch the boy's skin with my fingertips. A butterfly touch and his skin recoils automatically. Largest organ of the body with a life all its own. We draw back to the trolley and pore over his chart. He is wasting, has penile warts. The horror is I want to see them, run my lips over them in an intact, seronegative bravado. Challenge the reaper. Our power is paramount, we must choose not to be abusive. Her thin fingers mark it and we talk about time. The year I was an incendiary expert for the IRA. Five years from infection to finish. A blaze of night sweats. Violet and crimson, gold streaking out into the atmosphere and then nothing. A spent firework cumulus of smoke drifts to earth. And a few more months for this boy in the comfort of the witch-doctor. There is a blue pulse in her neck, below ear lobe, left of jaw hinge. Thin blood, a flat, gold chain undulates over clavicle. In the tenth bed, a man who thinks he might be twenty-five coughs sputum threaded red into the metal, kidney-shaped bowl. A star burst of death. A living fetus in the chicken egg yolk, in a Tupperware bowl at my parents' house when I was a child. She says he is only the second man she has ever seen wear pyjamas in this country. The striped wynciette bags over limbs, racked up to knees, the horny, thick, whitish skin around his ankles flakes and scatters. What is there in the depth of her eyes? How can I learn it in two minutes? The man's arms are break-thin, he has the look of the condemned, TB in the top of his chest. Eyes that should be white are yellow as they appeal to me, to anyone in the room who has the western promise and an intact immune system. H.I.V. positive. Full blown AIDS. In this room over half the men host the virus, multiplying like mutant frog spawn in the pond of their cells. We sit in the nurse's station. They bustle past us to a padlocked cupboard. Reach in for the clear glass bottles of medication. The same needle for every patient. The walls are sickly yellow in their attempt to crowd me. The floor makes a move. She is talking hopelessness. There is a gap between her front teeth, a slight overbite. I am moved to cup her head, to run the flesh pad of my thumbs across her closed eyelids. But we are up and walking. The same grey/yellow concrete, past cauldrons of bubbling nzima and chinese greens. Steaming into the firmament. The women smiling in boot-polish mahogany skin as ebony, the carved years in their faces. Blur of primary colours, patterns from the lake, from the sea. And the sun moves towards me like a soldier. Its force unrequited, unremitting. I am shaking her hand on the steps of the entrance. The red rubber of her stethoscope bleeds worm-like on yellow. Heat transference through our bodies. And when she has gone my hand still sings.

Other titles from Insomniac Press:

Room Behavior by Rob Kovitz
(cultural studies/architecture/non-fiction)

A woman sits alone in a darkened boiler-room. A man enjoys hanging suspended from the ceiling. A dirty room indicates the secret sexual proclivities of its occupant. A curtain rustling in the breeze portends fear and paranoia.

"The purpose of a room derives from the special nature of a room. A room is inside. This is what people in rooms have to agree on, as differentiated from lawns, meadows, fields, orchards."

Room Behavior is a book about rooms. Composed of texts and images from the most varied sources, including crime novels, decorating manuals, anthropological studies, performance art, crime scene photos, literature, and the Bible, Kovitz shapes the material through a process of highly subjective editing and juxtaposition to create an original, fascinating and darkly funny rumination about the behavior of rooms and the people that they keep.

5 1/2" x 7 1/2" • 288 pages • trade paperback (162 B&W photos) • isbn 1-895837-44-8
Canada $19.99/U.S. $15.99/U.K. £11.99

The War In Heaven by Kent Nussey

The War In Heaven collects the latest work from Kent Nussey. A unique blend of the stark realism of Raymond Carver and the lyrical precision of Russell Banks, Nussey's writing levels the mythologies of an urban paradise with fictions that are humorous but dark, touching and dangerous. In this book nothing is sacred, secure, or safe. Comprised of seven stories and a novella, *The War in Heaven* explores the human capacity for desire and destruction in a world where everything condenses beyond metaphor into organic connection. For Nussey love is the catalyst, creating the currents which sweep over his complex and provocative characters, and carry the reader to the brink of personal and historical apocalypse.

5 1/4" x 8 1/4" • 192 pages • trade paperback withflaps • isbn 1-895837-42-1
Canada $18.99/U.S. $13.99/U.K. £10.99

Dying for Veronica by Matthew Remski

A love story of bizarre proportions, Matthew Remski's first novel is set in Toronto. *Dying for Veronica* is a gritty and mysterious book, narrated by a man haunted by a twisted and unhappy childhood and obsessed with the sister he loves. This shadowy past explodes into an even more psychologically disturbing present — an irresistible quest and a longing that can not be denied. Remski's prose is beautiful, provocative, poetic: rich with the dark secrets and intricacies of Catholic mythology as it collides with, and is subsumed by, North American culture.

5 1/4" x 8 1/4" • 224 pages • trade paperback withflaps • isbn 1-895837-40-5
Canada $18.99/U.S. $14.99/U.K. £10.99

Carnival: a Scream In High Park reader edited by Peter McPhee

One evening each July an open-air literary festival is held in Toronto's High Park. It is a midway of diverse voices joined in celebration of poetry and story telling. Audiences exceeding 1,200 people gather under the oak trees to hear both well known and emerging writers from across the country, such as, Lynn Crosbie, Claire Harris, Steven Heighton, Nicole Brossard, Nino Ricci, Al Purdy, Susan Musgrave, Leon Rooke, Christopher Dewdney, Barbara Gowdy, bill bissett... This book collects the work (much of it new and previously unpublished) from the 48 writers who have performed at Scream in High Park in its first three years.

5 1/4" x 8 1/4" • 216 pages • trade paperback withflaps • isbn 1-895837-38-3
Canada $18.99/U.S. $14.99/U.K. £10.99

Beneath the Beauty by Phlip Arima

Beneath the Beauty is Phlip Arima's first collection of poetry. His work is gritty and rhythmic, passionate and uncompromising. His writing reveals themes like love, life on the street and addiction. Arima has a terrifying clarity of vision in his portrayal of contemporary life. Despite the cruelties inflicted and endured by his characters, he is able to find a compassionate element even in the bleakest of circumstances. Arima has a similar aesthetic to Charles Bukowski, but there is a sense of hope and dark romanticism throughout his work. Phlip Arima is a powerful poet and storyteller, and his writing is not for the faint of heart.

5 1/4" x 8 1/4" • 80 pages • trade paperback • isbn 1-895837-36-7
Canada $11.99/U.S. $9.99/U.K. £7.99

What Passes for Love by Stan Rogal

What Passes for Love is a collection of short stories which show the dynamics of male-female relationships. These ten short stories by Stan Rogal resonate with many aspects of the mating rituals of men and women: paranoia, obsession, voyeurism, and assimilation. Stan Rogal's first collection of stories, *What Passes for Love*, is an intriguing search through many relationships, and the emotional turmoil within them. Stan's writing reflects the honesty and unsentimentality, previously seen in his two books of poetry and published stories. Throughout *What Passes for Love* are paintings by Kirsten Johnson.

5 1/4" x 8 1/4" • 144 pages • trade paperback • isbn 1-895837-34-0
Canada $14.99/U.S. $12.99/U.K. £8.99

Bootlegging Apples on the Road to Redemption
by Mary Elizabeth Grace

This is Grace's first collection of poetry. It is an exploration of the collective self, about all of us trying to find peace; this is a collection of poetry about searching for the truth of one's story and how it is never heard or told, only experienced. It is the second story: our attempts with words to express the sounds and images of the soul. Her writing is soulful, intricate and lyrical. The book comes with a companion CD of music/poetry compositions which are included in the book.

5 1/4" x 8 1/4" • 80 pages • trade paperback with cd • isbn 1-895837-30-8
Canada $21.99/U.S. $19.99/U.K. £13.99

The Last Word: an insomniac anthology of canadian poetry
edited by michael holmes

The Last Word is a snapshot of the next generation of Canadian poets, the poets who will be taught in schools — voices reflecting the '90s and a new type of writing sensibility. The anthology brings together 51 poets from across Canada, reaching into different regional, ethnic, sexual and social groups. This varied and volatile collection pushes the notion of an anthology to its limits, like a startling Polaroid. Proceeds from the sale of *The Last Word* will go to Frontier College, in support of literacy programs across Canada.

5 1/4" x 8 1/4" • 168 pages • trade paperback • isbn 1-895837-32-4
Canada $16.99/U.S. $12.99/U.K. £9.99

Desire High Heels Red Wine
Timothy Archer, Sky Gilbert, Sonja Mills and Margaret Webb

Sweet, seductive, dark and illegal; this is *Desire, High Heels, Red Wine*, a collection by four gay and lesbian writers. The writing ranges from the abrasive comedy of Sonja Mills to the lyrical and insightful poetry of Margaret Webb, from the campy dialogue of Sky Gilbert to the finely crafted short stories of Timothy Archer. Their writings depict dark, abrasive places populated by bitch divas, leather clad bodies, and an intuitive sense of sexuality and gender. The writers' works are brought together in an elaborate and striking design by three young designers.

5 1/4" x 8 1/4" • 96 pages • trade paperback • isbn 1-895837-26-X
Canada $12.99/U.S. $9.99/U.K. £7.99

Beds & Shotguns
Diana Fitzgerald Bryden, Paul Howell McCafferty, Tricia Postle & Death Waits

Beds & Shotguns is a metaphor for the extremes of love. It is also a collection by four emerging poets who write about the gamut of experiences between these opposites from romantic to obsessive, fantastic to possessive. These poems and stories capture love in its broadest meanings and are set against a dynamic, lyrical landscape.

5 1/4" x 8 1/4" • 96 pages • trade paperback • isbn 1-895837-28-6
Canada $13.99/U.S. $10.99/U.K. £7.99

Playing in the Asphalt Garden
Phlip Arima, Jill Battson, Tatiana Freire-Lizama and Stan Rogal

This book features new Canadian urban writers, who express the urban experience — not the city of buildings and streets, but as a concentration of human experience, where a rapid and voluminous exchange of ideas, messages, power and beliefs takes place.

5 3/4" x 9" • 128 pages • trade paperback • isbn 1-895837-20-0
Canada $14.99/U.S. $10.99/U.K. £9.99

Mad Angels and Amphetamines
Nik Beat, Mary Elizabeth Grace, Noah Leznoff and Matthew

A collection by four emerging Canadian writers and three graphic designers. In this book, design is an integral part of the prose and poetry. Each writer collaborated with a designer so that the graphic design is an interpretation of the writer's works. Nik Beat's lyrical and unpretentious poetry Noah Leznoff's darkly humorous prose and narrative poetic cycles; Mary Elizabeth Grace's Celtic dialogues and mysti cal images; and Matthew Remski's medieval symbols and surrealistic style of story; this is the mixture of styles that weave together in *Mad Angels and Amphetamines*.

6" x 9" • 96 pages • trade paperback • isbn 1-895837-14-6
Canada $12.95/U.S. $9.95/U.K. £8.99

Insomniac Press • 378 Delaware Ave.
Toronto, Ontario, Canada • M6H 2T8
phone: (416) 536-4308 • fax: (416) 588-4198
email: insomna@pathcom.com